BOSTON
ENGLISH
Illustrated

Dana Lynn Wilson

With *photography* by DOSS/NATALE

CENTENNIAL PRESS • LINCOLN

ABOUT THE AUTHOR

DANA LYNN WILSON is a freelance writer and photographer who lives in Brookline, Massachusetts. She is a descendant of Josiah Bartlett, a Revolutionary patriot who signed the Declaration of Independence and became the first governor of New Hampshire.

Her writing has appeared in numerous newspapers and magazines in the United States and abroad. Her syndicated column, "Nine to Five," is about what people do for a living.

Photograph by Lynn McCann

DANA LYNN WILSON

ISBN 0-8220-1633-8

© Copyright 1976 by Centennial Press
Printed in U.S.A. All Rights Reserved.
Centennial Press is a division of
Cliffs Notes, Inc., Box 80728, Lincoln, Nebraska, 68501.

Pleashaw—state or feeling of being pleased. "I don't remembah our being introduced, but it's a *pleashaw* to meet yuh."

Moa—the opposite of less and rhymes with boa. "Foa *moa*, please?"

Bawn—brought forth by birth. "Being *bawn* in Bawhston isn't a mattah of life and death. It's moa impawtant."

Pock—to place a vehicle in a stationary position. "What do yuh mean I cahn't triple-*pock* my cah? This is Bawhston isn't it?"

Shut—a garment for the upper torso, typically with sleeves and collar. "This *shut* hahse bean in the family for generations."

Ouwah—a unit of sixty minutes of time. "I've bean waiting an *ouwah* for yuh."

Goggle—mouthwash. "A salt wotta *goggle* is excellent for a soa throat."

Otter—a command. "Yuh bettah follow the doctah's *otters.*"

Motch — to walk to a military cadence. "History outside of Bawhston? The Minutemen didn't *motch* on Broadway, did they?"

Awnt—the wife of an uncle. "My *awnt*'s a Cabot. Who's yuhr's?"

Lodge—the opposite of small. "Ah yuh referring to my feet as *lodge*?"

Impawtant—significant, noteworthy. "Of course, Benjamin Franklin was an *impawtant* man. He was bawn in Bawhston."

Waw—a conflict carried on by force of arms. "The *Waw* of Independence was stotted by the Stamp Act."

Shock—a large, ferocious marine fish. "Ah, ha, ha, ha! Yuh cahn't get a *shock* in fresh wotta."

Awt—the quality, production, or expression according to aesthetic principles of what is beautiful. "I've hud theyah's places called *awt* museums outside of Bawhston. But do they hahve *awt*?"

Bach—the sound a dog makes. "That dog's *bach* is awful."

Pawn—the abbreviation for obscene literature. "We don't ban *pawn* in Bawhston. We civilize it."

Shop—shrewd, astute. "If yuh're so *shop*, wheyah's yuhr school tie?"

Weathuh—the state of the atmosphere defined by temperature, moisture, wind velocity, and pressure. "The *weathuh*? Now theyah's a stimulating topic."

Gull—a young female. "They didn't allow *gulls* in Hahvod in my day!"

Cod – a small, flat piece of stiff paperboard for playing bridge and other games. "I sawr that *cod* up yuhr sleeve."

Alahm—a call to arms or warning of danger. "And then Paul Revere rode out to sound the *alahm*."

Faughty—the number between 39 and 41. "We'll discuss promotions when yuh're *faughty*."

Such—to make a probe or careful investigation. "*Such* the records. My ancestahs didn't just sail on the *Mayflowah*. They built it."

Sauce — one that supplies information. "This awticle doesn't identify its *sauces*."

Cuber—the Caribbean island ruled by Fidel Castro.
"Havanner. Yuh know, on the seashaw of *Cuber*."

Hod—difficult. "Yes, it's *hod* to know if the streets or the buildings came fust in Bawhston. But anyone who was bawn heyah knows."

Cawn — a tall cereal grass with kernels on large ears. "No doubt the Pilgrims wuhdah stahved without *cawn*."

Caught—the room in which trials are held. "So what, if the judge's *caught* is without heating and lights. It has an historic plaque!"

Cotton—a cardboard box. "Oh, I nevah throw out an egg *cotton*. They may be valuable someday."

Cuppachowdah—a creamy stew of clams, potatoes, and onions served in a cup. "I ottered crackuhs with my *cuppachowdah*."

Hot—the muscular organ that pumps blood. "Mothah, don't break my *hot*! Everyone else approves of her."

Alogy — hypersensitive reaction to the environment. "Ahchoo! It's my *alogy* again."

Sot—a type or class of similar persons or things. "My fathuh was the *sot* who nevah drank."

Draw — a compartment in a chest for storing clothes.
"That smotts. Yuh closed the *draw* on my fingah."

Altah — to change. "*Altah* Bawhston? Nevah!"

Fauce – to impose an action through power or strength. "When it comes to membahship, we prefer our own sot at the Union Club. Yuh cahn't *faucet*."

Potty — a social gathering. "The Bawhston Tea *Potty* was a wawning to the British."

Dock—the opposite of light. "The lantons of the old Nawth Church bunned in the *dock* to alert the Minutemen."

Hahbah—a port for sheltering ships and boats. "I know yuh've a yawht ankodd in Bawhston *Hahbah*. But is it a Twelve-Meter?"

Drawering—a sketch made with pencil, pen, or crayon. "Eighteenth-century *drawerings*? Ahn't they a bit nouveau for our awt museum?"

Kneelee—almost. "Yuh *kneelee* shotchanged me a nickel!"

Dot—a small, slender missle, usually feathered at one end and pointed at the other. "Aim the *dots* at the dotbawd."

Sutton—definite, indisputable. "Oh, I'm *sutton* Abagail mayreed John Adams in the Weymouth Meeting House. My great-great-great grandfathuh was theyah."

Flaw — the surface of the room on which one stands. "I cahn covah any *flaw* with a rug."

Propuh — correct. "Is Bawhston the only place in Ameriker wheyah *propuh* English is spoken?"